Also by Jaroslaw Jankowski

Why Are We So Different?
Your Guide to the 16 Personality Types

Why are we so very different from one another?
Why do we organise our lives in such disparate
ways? Why are our modes of assimilating
information so varied? Why are our approaches
to decision-making so diverse? Why are our
forms of relaxing and 'recharging our batteries'
so dissimilar?

Your Guide to the 16 Personality Types will help you
to understand both yourselves and other people
better. It will aid you not only in avoiding any
number of traps, but also in making the most of
your personal potential, as well as in taking the
right decisions about your education and career
and in building healthy relationships with others.
The book contains the ID16$^{TM©}$ Personality
Test, which will enable you to determine your
own personality type. It also offers
a comprehensive description of each of the
sixteen types.

The Counsellor

Your Guide
to the ENFJ Personality Type

The ID16™© Personality Types series

JAROSLAW JANKOWSKI
M.Ed., EMBA

LOGOS MEDIA

This is a book which can help you exploit your potential more fully, build healthy relationships with other people and make the right decisions about your education and career. However, it should not be considered to be a substitute for expert physiological or psychiatric consultation. Neither the author nor the publisher accept any responsibility whatsoever for any detrimental effects which may result from the inappropriate use of this book.

ID16™© is an independent typology developed by Polish educator and manager Jaroslaw Jankowski and grounded in Carl Gustav Jung's theory. It should not be confused with the personality typologies and tests proposed by other authors or offered by other institutions.

Original title: Twój typ osobowości: Doradca (ENFJ)
Translated from the Polish by Caryl Swift
Proof reading: Lacrosse | experts in translation
Layout editing by Zbigniew Szalbot

Published by LOGOS MEDIA

Paperback: ISBN 978-83-7981-060-4
EPUB: ISBN 978-83-7981-061-1
MOBI: ISBN 978-83-7981-062-8

Contents

Preface

The work in your hands is a compendium of knowledge on the *counsellor*. It forms part of the *ID16*^{TM©} *Personality Types* series, which consists of sixteen books on the individual personality types and *Who Are You? The ID16*^{TM©} *Personality Test*, an introduction to the ID16^{TM©} independent personality typology, which is based on the theory developed by Carl Gustav Jung.

As you explore this book on the *counsellor*, you will find the answer to a number of crucial questions:

- How do *counsellors* think and what do they feel? How do they make decisions? How do they solve problems? What makes them anxious? What do they fear? What irritates them?

- Which personality types are they happy to encounter on their road through life and which ones do they avoid? What kind of friends, life partners and parents do they make? How do others perceive them?
- What are their vocational predispositions? What sort of work environment allows them to function most effectively? Which careers best suit their personality type?
- What are their strengths and what do they need to work on? How can they make the most of their potential and avoid pitfalls?
- Which famous people correspond to the *counsellor*'s profile?

The book also contains the most essential information about the ID16™© typology.

We sincerely hope that it will help you in coming to know yourself and others better.

ID16™© and Jungian Personality Typology

ID16™© numbers among what are referred to as Jungian personality typologies, which draw on the theories developed by Carl Gustav Jung (1875-19161), a Swiss psychiatrist and psychologist and a pioneer of the 'depth psychology' approach.

On the basis of many years of research and observation, Jung came to the conclusion that the differences in people's attitudes and preferences are far from random. He developed a concept which is highly familiar to us today: the division of people into extroverts and introverts. In addition, he distinguished four personality functions, which form two opposing pairs: sensing-intuition and thinking-feeling. He also established that one function is dominant in each pair. He became convinced that each and every person's dominant functions are fixed and independent of external conditions and that, together, what they form is a personality type.

In 1938, two American psychiatrists, Horace Gray and Joseph Wheelwright, created the first personality test based on Jung's theories. It was designed to make it possible to determine the dominant functions within the three dimensions described by Jung, namely, **extraversion-introversion**, **sensing-intuition** and **thinking-feeling**. That first test became the inspiration for other researchers. In 1942, again in America, Isabel Briggs Myers and Katherine Briggs began using their own personality test, broadening Gray's and Wheelwright's classic, three-dimensional model to include a fourth: **judging-perceiving**. The majority of subsequent personality typologies and tests drawing on Jung's theories also take that fourth dimension into account. They include the American typology published by David W. Keirsey in 1978 and the personality test developed in the nineteen seventies by Aušra Augustinavičiūtė, a Lithuanian psychologist. Over the following decades, other European researchers followed in their footsteps, creating more four-dimensional personality typologies and tests for use in personal coaching and career counselling.

ID16$^{TM©}$ figures among that group. An independent typology developed by Polish educator and manager Jaroslaw Jankowski, it was published in the first decade of the twenty-first century. ID16$^{TM©}$ is based on Carl Jung's classic theory and, like other contemporary Jungian typologies, it follows a four-dimensional path, terming those dimensions the **four natural inclinations**. These inclinations are dichotomous in nature and the picture they provide gives us information regarding a person's personality type. Analysis of the first inclination is intended to determine the dominant **source of life energy**, this being either the exterior or the interior world. Analysis of the second inclination defines the dominant **mode of assimilating information**, which occurs via the senses or via intuition. Analysis of the third inclination supplies a description of the **decision-making mode**, where either mind or heart is dominant, while analysis of the fourth inclination produces a definition of the dominant **lifestyle** as either organised or spontaneous. The combination of all these natural inclinations results in **sixteen possible personality types**.

One remarkable feature of the ID16™© typology is its practical dimension. It describes the individual personality types in action – at work, in daily life and in interpersonal relations. It neither concentrates on the internal dynamics of personality nor does it undertake any theoretical attempts at explaining or commenting on invisible, interior processes. The focus is turned more toward the ways in which a given personality type manifests itself externally and how it affects the surrounding world. This emphasis on the social aspect of personality places ID16™© somewhat closer to the previously mentioned typology developed by Aušra Augustinavičiūtė.

Each of the ID16™© personality types is the result of a given person's natural inclinations.

There is nothing evaluative or judgemental about ascribing a person to a given type, though. No particular personality type is 'better' or 'worse' than any other. Each type is quite simply different and each has its own potential strengths and weaknesses. ID16™© makes it possible to identify and describe those differences. It helps us to understand ourselves and discover our place in the world.

Familiarity with our personality profile enables us to make full use of our potential and work on the areas which might cause us trouble. It is an invaluable aid in everyday life, in solving problems, in building healthy relationships with other people and in making decisions relating to our education and careers.

Determining personality is a process which is neither arbitrary nor mechanical in nature. As the 'owner and user' of our personality, each and every one of us is fully capable of defining which type we belong to. The individual's role is thus pivotal. This self-identification can be achieved either by analysing the descriptions of the ID16™© personality types and steadily narrowing down the fields of choice or by taking the short cut provided by the ID16™© Personality Test.[1] The role played by each 'personality user' is equally crucial when it comes to the test, given that the outcome depends entirely on the answers they provide.

---

[1] The test can be found in *Why Are We So Different? Your Guide to the 16 Personality Types* by Jaroslaw Jankowski.

Identifying personality types helps us to know both ourselves and others. Nonetheless, it should not be treated as some kind of future-determining oracle. No personality type can ever justify our weaknesses or poor interpersonal relationships. It might, however, help us to understand their causes!

ID16™© treats personality type not as a static, genetic, pre-determined condition, but as a product of innate and acquired characteristics. As such, it is a concept which neither diminishes free will nor engages in pigeonholing people. What it does is open up new perspectives for us, encouraging us to work on ourselves and indicating the areas where that work is most needed.

The Counsellor (ENFJ)

THE ID16™© PERSONALITY TYPOLOGY

The Personality in a Nutshell

Life motto: My friends are my world

In brief, *counsellors* …

are optimistic, enthusiastic and quick-witted. Courteous and tactful, they have an extraordinary gift for empathy and find joy in acting for the good of others, with no thought of themselves. They have the ability to influence other people, inspiring them, eliciting their hidden potential and giving them faith in their own powers. Radiating warmth, they draw others to them and often help them in solving their personal problems.

Counsellors can be over-trusting and have a tendency to view the world through rose-tinted glasses. With their focus on other people, they often forget about their own needs.

The *counsellor's* four natural inclinations:

- source of life energy: the exterior world
- mode of assimilating information: intuition
- decision-making mode: the heart
- lifestyle: organised

Similar personality types:

- the Enthusiast
- the Mentor
- the Idealist

Statistical data:

- *counsellors* constitute between three and five per cent of the global community
- women predominate among *counsellors* (80 per cent)
- France is an example of a nation corresponding to the *counsellor's* profile[2]

---

[2] What this means is not that all the residents of France fall within this personality type, but that French society as a whole possesses a great many of the character traits typical of the *counsellor*.

The Four-Letter Code

In terms of Jungian personality typology, the universal four-letter code for the *counsellor* is ENFJ.

General character traits

Counsellors are energetic, nimble-witted and optimistic. They find joy in helping others and excel at reading their feelings and emotions. When they observe people, they spot things that remain hidden to others. With their extraordinary intuition and empathy, they are capable of lifting other people's spirits, inspiring them and motivating them to act.

Attitude to others

Counsellors have a healthy sense of their own worth, but are ready to surrender their needs and adapt to others if doing so will enable them to provide the necessary help or support. The problems experienced by their family and friends affect them deeply and they are often so focused on other people that they have no time to reflect on their own lives. Indeed, sometimes they even have difficulty in defining their personal aims in life or their needs.

Others perceive them as superb teachers and mentors and as people in whom they can confide, appreciating them for their help and turning to them for advice in difficult situations. By profession, *counsellors* are often providers of good counsel … hence the name for this personality type. Nevertheless, regardless of what they do for a living, they will be a source of such counsel for their friends and relations and will often help them to solve their personal problems. Their insights, which strike *counsellors* themselves as absolutely natural and self-evident, are a source of tremendous inspiration to others and prompt them to view a situation with a fresh eye and in a new way.

Although other people's problems absorb a considerable amount of their time, the awareness that they can help someone gives *counsellors* immense joy. In general, they feel responsible for others and find it impossible to stand indifferently by in the face of another person's troubles. At times, they might try to improve other people's lives whether they want it or not, or to do everything for them.

Thinking and perception

Counsellors' thoughts are turned towards the future and they rarely reflect on past failures. Their thinking is global and far-reaching and they derive joy not only from accomplishing their plans, but also from the very process of planning and then proceeding towards the goal. The future excites them more than the present and they look at problems from a broad perspective, perceiving various aspects of the issues they are involved with. They also have an inbuilt capability to multitask.

Counsellors dream of a better world and believe in the possibility of turning those dreams into reality. Their vision spurs them to act and injects them with energy. In general, they like change and new challenges and adopt innovative concepts and ideas with an enthusiasm which can, at times, be indiscriminating. They are often interested in the reality of the spirit and social problems also move them. By nature, *counsellors* are egalitarians. On occasion, they might well subordinate their lives to one idea and work to accomplish it in a way which is almost fanatical.

Interior compass

Counsellors follow the values they profess in life and are mistrustful of decisions taken solely on the basis of logical and rational arguments. When someone attacks their system of values or behaves in a manner which affronts their convictions, they are capable of protesting sharply, much to the astonishment of those around them, since their usual tendency is to step aside for others and avoid confrontations. In extreme cases, they are even ready to take up cudgels and fight for what seems to them to be right and just. However, given that they are, by nature, inclined to leave their own rights bringing up the rear, it will be a fight in defence of principles and standards of behaviour which, in their opinion, are incontrovertible.

As others see them

As a rule, *counsellors* are widely liked and have an uncommon power to draw others to them. Even the coldest and most rigorously conservative of people rarely remain indifferent to their charm, warmth, sincerity and wide range of interests. They are considered to be people who can always be counted on. Their advice helps others to see problems in a new light and talking to them spurs people to act and augments their faith in their own powers. To some people, though, the *counsellor's* optimism seems suspect, while they themselves appear overly enthusiastic and out of touch with reality, sometimes even to the point of naïvety and gullibility.

Counsellors, in turn, are irritated by scepticism in others, as well as by chronic pessimism, lethargy, stagnant attitudes and a lack of faith in the potential for change. They find those who indifferently pass by another person's suffering and ignore the feelings of others incomprehensible. In their eyes, a life devoted only to satisfying one's own needs is a life impoverished and devoid of values. Equally as bewildering to them are people for whom an atmosphere of harmony and warmth is of no account, as are those who consciously pursue confrontation. They themselves are highly sensitive to criticism and will do anything they can to avoid conflicts and unpleasant situations.

Communication

Counsellors display extraordinary tact and intuition in their interpersonal communication. They are masters of the diplomatic, with the gift of always knowing what to say in a given situation and an ability to influence people, shape their behaviour and even to manipulate them when the cause is a good one. As a rule, they are highly communicative and persuasive.

They prefer to communicate directly and orally. Being well aware of the immense power of words, they keep the language they use under firm control. Indeed, they will sometimes give prior thought to what to say in a given situation and, when an essential conversation awaits them, they may even play it out in their minds first. They are usually unafraid of speaking in public and have the ability to present their viewpoints clearly and comprehensibly. There is one exception to this, though. When they evoke the values they profess, they mistakenly assume that they are generally shared by other people and then what they are saying can often be obscure.

In the face of conflict

As *counsellors* see it, healthy relations with other people are the key to happiness in life and at work. When they are aware of an unresolved conflict, they are unable to function normally within their family or focus on what they are doing at work. With their need for warmth, acceptance, endearment and sincerity, they also dislike being alone. Nevertheless, since they derive joy from giving, they are capable of living a happy life even when their needs are unmet.

Their exceptionally low threshold of tolerance for criticism and tendency to avoid any and every kind of unpleasant situation mean that they will often surrender in the face of conflict, either giving up the fight entirely or agreeing to unfavourable conditions simply in order to put an end to an uncomfortable situation. Unfortunately though, in taking that course of action, they expose themselves to similar, equally distressing experiences in the future.

Challenges

Counsellors usually lead active lives and rarely have time to relax. In their free time, they are frequently involved in activities geared towards helping either society or their friends and acquaintances. This may give them great joy, but their low assertiveness and inability to say 'no' means that they take on too many responsibilities and are often overburdened as a result. With their desire to respond to every need that arises, they are frequently distracted and they lack the ability to focus on priorities.

They like being among people, but are highly sensitive and vulnerable to hurt. With their low threshold of tolerance for criticism, they take every unfavourable remark to heart and any unflattering comment whatsoever affects them deeply. By the same token, they are incapable of availing themselves of help from others. They find being alone for any length of time hard to bear, as well; when they are cut off from other people, they are swept by despondency and apathy.

Socially

Counsellors feel thoroughly at home among people. Social relationships are one of the most important things in their lives; they invest a great deal of energy in them and are unusually loyal. They value acceptance, honesty, intensity and warmth in interpersonal relations and are quicker than most to perceive the feelings, emotions and needs of others. Being exceptionally sensitive, they take coolness, indifference and criticism extremely badly.

As a rule, *counsellors* are very outgoing and friendly. They have the ability to express their emotions and feelings and readily share them with their friends. Their attitude to others is highly positive and enthusiastic; they believe in people and genuinely hope for their happiness, identifying with them and sharing in their joys and sorrows. They often feel the suffering of another almost to the point of physicality, while other people's joy means that they themselves are happy.

When they are among other people, they give them their full attention and it is rare indeed for them to focus on thrusting themselves forward or advertising their own points of view, although they are fully capable of articulating them clearly as and when the need arises.

Amongst friends

Counsellors are brimming with of energy and optimism and have an abundant and sparkling sense of humour. They are widely liked, draw others to them and can always be counted on. Their behaviour is natural, they are good listeners and are genuinely interested in other people's experiences and problems. All these qualities make them perfect friendship material. Their acceptance, understanding and sincere interest mean that the people in their company feel better about themselves and their worth.

Counsellors are extremely faithful friends and those who confide in them can be assured of their trustworthiness. They lift their friends' spirits and give them faith in their own powers, perceiving their hidden potential and making them aware of their inherent possibilities. They see helping their friends as something utterly natural and it gives them immense joy to do so. However, their positive attitude to others means that they are not always able to refuse them and they allow themselves to be used as a result.

They usually forge healthy and friendly relationships with everyone, regardless of personality type. However, they most frequently strike up a friendship with *enthusiasts*, *mentors*, *advocates* and other *counsellors* and, most rarely, with *practitioners*, *animators* and *inspectors*.

As life partners

Counsellors treat their relationship with their life partner as precisely that: a relationship for life. They bring a massive dose of warmth, tenderness and acceptance to it, along with their abundant sense of humour, and expect the same in return, suffering if their partners fail to show them love and affection. On the whole, though, they tend not to make too much of it, since they derive joy from giving and the happiness of their nearest and dearest will also be their happiness in some measure. They are faithful, loyal and exceptionally devoted.

Counsellors see the best in their partners, accepting them, supporting them and, on many an occasion, making excuses for them. However, the balance between giving and receiving in their relationships often slips out of kilter, given that, by nature, they give much more than they take. With their focus firmly on the happiness of their partner, they seldom fight for their own rights or shine a light on their own needs. They regularly 'monitor' the status of their mutual relationships and their partner's emotional state, for instance by asking how they are feeling, which some people may well find tiresome.

Their low threshold of tolerance for criticism is an ever-present problem for *counsellors*. Blunt remarks and direct comments from a less sensitive partner will hurt them and they will do anything they can to avoid conflicts and unpleasant conversations. In general, they would rather suffer than call other people's attention to their inappropriate behaviour and they also have problems in withdrawing from destructive relationships, often remaining in them for a very long time as a result. Faced with trouble in their relationship, they are ready to work at it and make sacrifices. If their efforts fail to produce results, they have a tendency to blame themselves for the lack of success and, if a relationship falls apart, they give their minds over to pondering the mistakes they made. However, on the whole, it will not be long before they shake themselves out of their reflections and come to terms with parting.

The natural candidates for a *counsellor's* life partner are people of a personality type akin to their own: *enthusiasts*, *mentors* or *idealists*. Building mutual understanding and harmonious relations will be easier in a union of that kind. Nonetheless, experience has taught us that people are also capable of creating happy and successful relationships despite what would seem to be an evident typological incompatibility.

As parents

Counsellors make responsible parents, taking their duties in this respect very seriously and being well aware of the importance of having proper relationships with their children. They endeavour to pass on the values which they themselves believe in and truly wish to be a good example. They show their children warmth, tenderness and care. Unstinting in their praise and words of encouragement, they accept them as they are and make that plain to them. Nonetheless, they are capable of applying discipline and inculcating their offspring with the standards and principles which give order to their world, since they earnestly wish for them both to perceive the difference between desirable and reprehensible behaviour and to be able to make the right choices. *Counsellor* parents take good care to ensure that their children want for nothing and they are a steady presence in their offspring's lives, empathising with them and, as and when the circumstances demand, offering comfort, encouragement, motivation or ideas. They will always be by their side at difficult moments and it is a rare event for them to miss the fact that they are wrestling with a problem.

Counsellors have the ability to influence their children's behaviour, something which they normally employ for worthy ends, such as increasing their faith in their own powers.

However, at times, they may attempt to manipulate them. They also have a tendency to do everything for them, thus depriving them of the chance to experiment and learn from their mistakes. At times, older children will complain that their *counsellor* parent is interfering too much in their lives and, fed up with parental over-protectiveness and what they perceive to be excessive control, they will occasionally envy their peers' freedom and lack of restrictions. Looking back, though, they are grateful to their *counsellor* parent for surrounding them with love, being their support and teaching them to distinguish right from wrong.

Work and career paths

Counsellors cope very well with change, are happy to learn something new and enjoy challenges. They are able to put their whole heart into accomplishing purposes they believe in. Although they have no fear of innovative tasks and pioneering ventures, they like order, structure, proper organisation and clear, comprehensible rules. Sparking their enthusiasm for work on a project when they are not properly prepared or where the aim is only fuzzily defined will be difficult. They prefer straightforward solutions and will thus do their best to simplify complicated procedures and strip complex systems down to the essentials. Good organisers themselves, they like working according to plan and take their responsibilities extremely seriously. When they make decisions, they take into consideration not only the relevant objective reasoning or the economic score, but also the potential impact on people's lives. In general, they believe that changes which will affect employees should be agreed with them or that there should, at the very least, be a consultation process.

As part of a team

Counsellors derive great satisfaction from jobs requiring contact with people and are happy to work in companies and institutions where the driving purpose is to solve human problems or improve lives. They are tailor-made for customer service departments and advice or welfare centres, coping excellently with tasks demanding interpersonal skills. When they work as part of a team, they are pillars of support for their colleagues; indeed, they go well beyond the call of duty in this respect.

Counsellors have the ability to create a warm, friendly atmosphere and to engender comprise, as well as having a positive influence on their colleagues, motivating them, inspiring them and infecting them with optimism and faith in their success. They are unhappy both in soulless corporations where the emotions, feelings and needs of the employees count for nothing and in institutions where people perform the function of 'cogs in the machine'. Open, honest, natural and direct relationships with their colleagues are crucial to them and they dislike environments where mutual contact between staff members is formalised and the exchange of information only takes place within rigorously defined procedures. They will have difficulty fitting in with teams dominated by cool, reticent employees and they also have no liking for tasks which demand a host of routine activities, adherence to detailed instructions and the processing of huge quantities of data. On the whole they are easily distracted; if someone diverts their attention from their work and asks for advice, they are capable of completely forgetting the task they were engaged in and giving themselves over absolutely to the conversation.

Views on workplace hierarchy

Counsellors appreciate superiors who behave in line with the principles they profess, give their subordinates freedom in accomplishing their tasks and respect their individual style of working. When they themselves are given a position of authority, which occurs quite frequently, they behave in the same way. In their case, working in management positions usually incurs a great deal of stress, since they not only have to confront unpleasant situations head on, while their nature dictates that they avoid them, but are also obliged to be guided primarily by the company's economic interests, something which will not always be favourable as far as their subordinates are concerned. They feel a tremendous sense of discomfort on this account. Their tendency to make decisions prematurely might also prove to be a potential source of problems.

Professions

Knowledge of our own personality profile and natural preferences provides us with invaluable help in choosing the optimal path in our professional careers. Experience has shown that, while *counsellors* are perfectly able to work and find fulfilment in a range of fields, their personality type naturally predisposes them to the following fields and professions:

- acting
- advisor
- clergy
- life coach
- consultant
- diplomat
- editor
- human resources
- manager
- marketing
- musician
- paramedic
- physician
- police officer
- politician
- psychiatrist
- physiotherapist
- psychologist
- public relations
- rehabilitation
- reporter
- sales representative
- scientist

- social welfare
- supervisor / head of a team
- teacher
- therapist
- tertiary educator
- travel agent
- vocational training
- writer

Potential strengths and weaknesses

Like any other personality type, *counsellors* have their potential strengths and weaknesses and this potential can be cultivated in a variety of ways. *Counsellors'* personal happiness and professional fulfilment depend on whether they make the most of the 'pluses' offered by their personality type and face up to its inherent dangers. Here, then, is a SUMMARY of those 'pluses' and dangers:

Potential strengths

Counsellors are energetic and optimistic. Loyal and faithful, they can always be relied on. They are conscientious, responsible, orderly and well-organised. Their thinking is global and far-reaching and they look at problems from a broad perspective, perceiving various aspects of the issues they are engaging with. They live in accordance with the values they profess and, when the situation demands, they will stand in their defence without regard for the consequences. They voice their feelings and emotions openly and have excellent oral skills, with the ability to express their thoughts intelligibly and persuasively. However, imposing their views on others is alien to them, as is making themselves the focal point. Their focus is on other people; *counsellors* give of their time unstintingly and are ready to adapt to others and their needs if doing so will enable them to provide help in solving their problems or changing their lives for the better.

They display extraordinary tact and intuition in their interpersonal communication and are masters of the diplomatic. Their 'people skills' are outstanding and they have an immense gift both for empathy and for perceiving the feelings and emotions of others. They are very open towards other people, with a genuine interest in their problems and a sincere eagerness to help. With their highly developed intuition and perceptiveness, they are able to divine other people's thoughts, intentions and motives and are also quick to spot problems in interpersonal relationships. Being people of compromise and endowed with the gift of persuasion, they have the ability to build understanding and play an instrumental part in finding solutions which are favourable to all concerned. They are quick-witted, courteous and full of humour.

Counsellors are also excellent conversationalists, with the rare skill of listening to other people and the ability to elicit the best in them, spotting potential and possibilities that have gone unremarked by others. Talking to *counsellors* inspires people to act, motivates them, lifts their spirits and sets them believing in their own powers.

Counsellors also have a natural gift for drawing others to them; they are sought-after friends and colleagues. Their charm, warmth and sincerity, their natural attitude of acceptance and their wide range of interests mean that others enjoy being in their company, which gives them a sense of worth and a feeling of being appreciated. They are also natural leaders; where they go, others will follow, infected by their vision and faith that the venture will succeed.

Potential weaknesses

Counsellors are characterised by an extreme optimism and idealism. They usually see reality through rose-tinted glasses and have a tendency to marginalise negative occurrences, limitations and dangers; indeed, they might well fail to spot them at all. They quite often lose touch with reality as far as their ideas are concerned and are liable to subordinate their entire life to accomplishing one ruling notion, a course of action which may well narrow their world and cramp their perceptions. They can be critical and suspicious of opinions and viewpoints which diverge significantly from their own. With their inclination to do too much for others and even, at times, to manipulate them, they can also be overprotective or invasive.

Counsellors cope very badly with situations of conflict and have an exceptionally low threshold of tolerance for criticism levelled at them by others. They often prefer to keep quiet about their troubles or someone else's inappropriate behaviour rather than engage in a difficult conversation about the problem. They will do everything within their power to avoid unpleasant situations and their tendency to throw in the towel prematurely, yield and give up the fight for their own rights may manifest itself as a result. Ending destructive and toxic relationships is also something which frequently causes them difficulty. They have little appreciation for their own achievements and play down their role in successes; on the other hand, they are inclined to pin the blame for failures on themselves. They can have problems with accommodating themselves to socially accepted norms and conventions.

As a rule, *counsellors* are rather inflexible and find situations demanding improvisation hard to handle. They also have difficulty in making decisions on the basis of purely rational and logical premises, without reference to the social context. The awareness that a given decision may have an unfavourable impact on the lives of other people will often leave them paralysed and render them incapable of assessing a situation coolly and taking whatever action might be essential. The problems they sometimes have with carrying out objective evaluations stem from the same cause. Their sensitivity to the opinions and appraisals of others makes it difficult for them to function in an unfriendly environment and even more of a struggle in an outright hostile one. They incline towards perfectionism and this can reduce the efficacy of their activities, since they may well spend time improving things which suffice as they are. In general, they devote too little time to reflecting on their own lives and priorities and, in focusing on other people, they often forget about their own needs.

Personal development

Counsellors' personal development depends on the extent to which they make use of their natural potential and surmount the dangers inherent in their personality type. What follows are some practical tips which, together, form a specific guide that we might call *The Counsellor's Ten Commandments*.

Keep your focus fixed

You simply cannot help all of the people all of the time, any more than you can solve all of their problems. Keep your eyes firmly fixed on whatever is most crucial to you and stop letting yourself be distracted by less important matters. Do that and you will find yourself avoiding frustration and achieving more.

Stop fearing criticism

Quell your fear of expressing your own critical opinions and of accepting criticism from others. Criticism can be constructive. There is no law which says that it has to mean attacking people or undermining their worth.

Give some thought to yourself

Give some consideration to your own needs and find the time to reflect on your own life. Stop letting yourself be used and start learning to say 'no'. If you really want to help other people effectively, you also have to look after yourself.

Stop agonising over the plan and get going on the action

Instead of nit-picking over how you can improve on what you intend to do, simply get going and do it. Otherwise the day will come when you realise that you have spent your entire life perfecting your plans. Surely setting out to accomplish them and doing things well, but not necessarily to the point of sheer perfection, would be better than never doing anything at all?

Stop being afraid of conflict

Controversy does arise, even in our closest circles. Conflict need not necessarily be destructive. In fact, it very often helps us to identify problems and solve them! So, when conflicts emerge, stop hiding your head in the sand and, instead, express your point of view and feelings about the situation openly.

Be more practical

You have a natural inclination to come up with idealistic notions which sometimes have little in common with real life. Give some thought to the practical aspects and to how they can actually be accomplished in this imperfect world we live in.

Admit that you can make mistakes

None of us is infallible. Other people might well be absolutely right, or partially right and you might be partially or absolutely wrong. Accept that fact and learn to admit your mistakes.

Ask

Stop assuming that, if other people are silent, it means that they are indifferent or hostile. If you really want to know what they think, ask them.

Stop doing everything for others

Go ahead and help people to discover their potential and motivate them to act all you like – but then let them get on with it. You cannot live their lives for them, so allow them to take matters into their own hands, do things for themselves and learn from their own mistakes.

Take some time out

Try to get away from your responsibilities and duties once in a while and do something for the sheer pleasure, relaxation and fun of it. It will help you get a better perspective on things and when you go back to your tasks your mind and your thinking will be refreshed.

Well-known figures

Below is a list of some well-known people who match the *counsellor's* profile:

- **Abraham Maslow** (1908-1970); an American psychologist and the creator of 'Maslow's Hierarchy of Needs', he is considered to be one of the most important figures in the development of humanistic and transpersonal psychology.

- **Abraham Lincoln** (1809-1865); the 16th president of the United States.
- **Ronald Reagan** (1911-2004); the 40th president of the United States.
- **François Mitterrand** (1916-1996); the 21st president of France, he held office from 1981 to 1995.
- **Pope John Paul II** (Karol Jozef Wojtyla; 1920-2005); a Polish Roman Catholic priest, he became Archbishop of Krakow in 1964, was made a cardinal in 1967 and was elected to the papacy in 1978.
- **Sean Connery** (1930-2020); a Scottish screen actor whose filmography includes *The Name of the Rose*, he is the holder of numerous prestigious awards.
- **Mikhail Gorbachev** (1931-2022); a Russian politician and reformer, he was the last General Secretary of the Central Committee of the Communist Party of the Soviet Union and the one and only person to hold office as president of the USSR.
- **Tommy Lee Jones** (born in 1946); an American screen actor whose filmography includes *Men in Black*.
- **Samuel Leroy Jackson** (born in 1948); an American screen actor whose filmography includes *Jurassic Park*, he is also a producer.
- **Kirstie Alley** (1951-2022); an American screen actress and comedian whose filmography includes *Look Who's Talking*.
- **Patrick Swayze** (1952-2009); an American screen actor whose filmography

includes *Dirty Dancing*, he was also a dancer, singer and choreographer.

- **Tony Blair** (Anthony Charles Lynton Blair; born in 1953); a British politician and former leader of the Labour Party, he held office as prime minister of the United Kingdom three times in succession.
- **Barack Obama** (born in 1961); the 44th president of the United States.
- **Johnny Depp**, (John Christopher Depp II; born in 1963); an American screen actor whose filmography includes *Pirates of the Caribbean*.
- **Ben Stiller** (born in 1965); an American screen actor whose movies include *Meet the Fockers*, he is also a producer and director.

The ID16™© Personality Types in a Nutshell

The Administrator (ESTJ)

Life motto: We'll get the job done!

Administrators are hard-working, responsible and extremely loyal. Energetic and decisive, they value order, stability, security and clear rules. They are matter-of-fact and businesslike, logical, rational and practical and possess the capability to assimilate large amounts of detailed information.

Superb organisers, they are intolerant of ineffectuality, wastefulness and slothfulness. True to their convictions and direct in their contact with others, they present their point of view decisively and openly express critical opinions, sometimes hurting other people as a result.

The *administrator*'s four natural inclinations:

- source of life energy: the exterior world
- mode of assimilating information: via the senses
- decision-making mode: the mind
- lifestyle: organised

Similar personality types:

- the Animator
- the Inspector
- the Practitioner

Statistical data:

- *administrators* constitute between ten and thirteen per cent of the global community
- men predominate among *administrators* (60 per cent)
- the United States is an example of a nation corresponding to the *administrator's* profile[3]

Find out more!

The Administrator. Your Guide to the ESTJ Personality Type by Jaroslaw Jankowski

---

[3] What this means is not that all the residents of the USA fall within this personality type, but that American society as a whole possesses a great many of the character traits typical of the *administrator.*

The Advocate (ESFJ)

Life motto: How can I help you?

Advocates are well-organised, energetic and enthusiastic. Practical, responsible and conscientious, they are sincere and exceptionally gregarious.

Advocates are perceptive of human feelings, emotions and needs. They value harmony and find criticism and conflict difficult to bear. With their sensitivity to any and every manifestation of injustice, prejudice or detriment to another, they are genuinely interested in other people's problems and take real delight in helping them and tending to their needs, while often neglecting their own. They have a tendency to do everything for others and can be vulnerable to manipulation.

The *advocate*'s four natural inclinations:

- source of life energy: the exterior world
- mode of assimilating information: via the senses
- decision-making mode: the heart
- lifestyle: organised

Similar personality types:

- the Presenter
- the Protector
- the Artist

Statistical data:

- *advocates* constitute between ten and thirteen per cent of the global community
- women predominate among *advocates* (70 per cent)
- Canada is an example of a nation corresponding to the *advocate's* profile

Find out more!

The Advocate. Your Guide to the ESFJ Personality Type by Jaroslaw Jankowski

The Animator (ESTP)

Life motto: Let's DO something!

Animators are energetic, active and enterprising. Fond of the company of others, they have the ability to enjoy the moment and are spontaneous, flexible and open to change.

Animators are inspirers and instigators, spurring others to act. Being logical, rational and pragmatic realists, they are wearied by abstract concepts and solutions for the future. Their focus is on solving concrete problems in the here and now. They have difficulties with organising and planning and can be impulsive, acting first and thinking later.

The *animator's* four natural inclinations:

- source of life energy: the exterior world
- mode of assimilating information: via the senses

- decision-making mode: the mind
- lifestyle: spontaneous

Similar personality types:

- the Administrator
- the Practitioner
- the Inspector

Statistical data:

- *animators* constitute between six and ten per cent of the global community
- men predominate among *animators* (60 per cent)
- Australia is an example of a nation corresponding to the *animator's* profile

Find out more!

The Animator. Your Guide to the ESTP Personality Type by Jaroslaw Jankowski

The Artist (ISFP)

Life motto: Let's create something!

Artists are sensitive, creative and original, with a sense of the aesthetic and natural artistic talents. Independent in character, they follow their own system of values and are optimistic in outlook, with a positive approach to life and an ability to enjoy the moment.

Helping others is a source of joy to them. They find abstract theories tedious and would rather create reality than talk about it, although starting on something new comes more easily to them than finishing what they have already started. They have difficulty in voicing their own desires and needs.

The *artist's* four natural inclinations:

- source of life energy: the interior world
- mode of assimilating information: via the senses
- decision-making mode: the heart
- lifestyle: spontaneous

Similar personality types:

- the Protector
- the Presenter
- the Advocate

Statistical data:

- *artists* constitute between six and nine per cent of the global community
- women predominate among *artists* (60 per cent)
- China is an example of a nation corresponding to the *artist's* profile

Find out more!

The Artist. Your Guide to the ISFP Personality Type by Jaroslaw Jankowski

The Counsellor (ENFJ)

Life motto: My friends are my world

Counsellors are optimistic, enthusiastic and quick-witted. Courteous and tactful, they have an extraordinary gift for empathy and find joy in acting for the good of others, with no thought of themselves. They have the ability to influence other people, inspiring them, eliciting their hidden potential and giving them faith in their own powers. Radiating warmth, they draw others to them and often help them in solving their personal problems.

Counsellors can be over-trusting and have a tendency to view the world through rose-tinted glasses. With their focus on other people, they often forget about their own needs.

The *counsellor's* four natural inclinations:

- source of life energy: the exterior world
- mode of assimilating information: intuition
- decision-making mode: the heart
- lifestyle: organised

Similar personality types:

- the Enthusiast
- the Mentor
- the Idealist

Statistical data:

- *counsellors* constitute between three and five per cent of the global community
- women predominate among *counsellors* (80 per cent)
- France is an example of a nation corresponding to the *counsellor's* profile

Find out more!

The Counsellor. Your Guide to the ENFJ Personality Type by Jaroslaw Jankowski

The Director (ENTJ)

Life motto: I'll tell you what you need to do.

Directors are independent, active and decisive. Rational, logical and creative, when they analyse problems they look at the wider picture and are able to foresee the future consequences of human activities. They are characterised by optimism and a healthy sense of their own worth and are capable of transforming theoretical concepts into concrete, practical plans of action.

Visionaries, mentors and organisers, *directors* possess natural leadership skills. Their powerful personalities and direct and critical style can often have an intimidating effect, causing them problems in their interpersonal relationships.

The *director's* four natural inclinations:

- source of life energy: the exterior world

- mode of assimilating information: intuition
- decision-making mode: the mind
- lifestyle: organised

Similar personality types:

- the Innovator
- the Strategist
- the Logician

Statistical data:

- *directors* constitute between two and five per cent of the global community
- men predominate among *directors* (70 per cent)
- Holland is an example of a nation corresponding to the *director's* profile

Find out more!

The Director. Your Guide to the ENTJ Personality Type by Jaroslaw Jankowski

The Enthusiast (ENFP)

Life motto: We'll manage!

Enthusiasts are energetic, enthusiastic and optimistic. Capable of enjoying life and looking ahead to the future, they are dynamic, quick-witted and creative. They have a liking for people in general, value honest and genuine relationships and are warm, sincere and emotional. Criticism is something they handle badly. With their gift for empathy and ability to perceive people's needs, feelings and motives, they both inspire others and infect them with their own enthusiasm.

They love to be at the centre of events and are flexible and capable of improvising. Their inclination leads towards idealistic notions. Being easily distracted, they have problems with seeing things through to the end.

The *enthusiast's* four natural inclinations:

- source of life energy: the exterior world
- mode of assimilating information: intuition
- decision-making mode: the heart
- lifestyle: spontaneous

Similar personality types:

- the Counsellor
- the Idealist
- the Mentor

Statistical data:

- *enthusiasts* constitute between five and eight per cent of the global community
- women predominate among *enthusiasts* (60 per cent)
- Italy is an example of a nation corresponding to the *enthusiast's* profile

Find out more!

The Enthusiast. Your Guide to the ENFP Personality Type by Jaroslaw Jankowski

The Idealist (INFP)

Life motto: We CAN live differently.

Idealists are sensitive, loyal, and creative. Living in accordance with the values they hold is of immense importance to them and they both manifest an interest in the reality of the spirit and delve deeply into the mysteries of life. Wrapped up in the world's problems and open to the needs of other people, they prize harmony and balance.

Idealists are romantic; not only are they able to show love, but they also need warmth and affection themselves. With their outstanding ability to read other people's feelings and emotions, they build healthy, profound and enduring relationships. They feel that they are on very shaky ground in situations of conflict and have no real resistance to stress and criticism.

The *idealist's* four natural inclinations:

- source of life energy: the interior world
- mode of assimilating information: intuition
- decision-making mode: the heart
- lifestyle: spontaneous

Similar personality types:

- the Mentor
- the Enthusiast
- the Counsellor

Statistical data:

- *idealists* constitute between one and four per cent of the global community
- women predominate among *idealists* (60 per cent)
- Thailand is an example of a nation corresponding to the *idealist's* profile

Find out more!

The Idealist. Your Guide to the INFP Personality Type by Jaroslaw Jankowski

The Innovator (ENTP)

Life motto: How about trying a different approach…?

Innovators are inventive, original and independent. Optimistic, energetic and enterprising, they are people of action who love being at the centre of events and solving 'insoluble' problems. Their thoughts are turned to the future and they are curious about the world and visionary by nature. Open to new concepts and ideas, they enjoy new experiences and experiments and have the ability to identify the connections between separate events.

Innovators are spontaneous, communicative and self-assured. However, they tend to overestimate their own possibilities and have problems with seeing things through to the end. They are also inclined to be impatient and to take risks.

The *innovator's* four natural inclinations:

- source of life energy: the exterior world
- mode of assimilating information: intuition
- decision-making mode: the mind
- lifestyle: spontaneous

Similar personality types:

- the Director
- the Logician
- the Strategist

Statistical data:

- *innovators* constitute between three and five per cent of the global community
- men predominate among *innovators* (70 per cent)
- Israel is an example of a nation corresponding to the *innovator's* profile

Find out more!

The Innovator. Your Guide to the ENTP Personality Type by Jaroslaw Jankowski

The Inspector (ISTJ)

Life motto: *Duty first.*

Inspectors are people who can always be counted on. Well-mannered, punctual, reliable, conscientious and responsible, when they give their word, they keep it. Being analytical, methodical, systematic and logical by nature, they tend be seen as serious, cold and reserved. They prize calm, stability and order, have no fondness for change and like clear principles and concrete rules.

Inspectors are hard-working, persevering and capable of seeing things through to the end. As perfectionists, they try to exercise control over everything within their sphere and are sparing in their praise. They also underrate the importance of other people's feelings and emotions.

The *inspector's* four natural inclinations:

- source of life energy: the interior world
- mode of assimilating information: via the senses
- decision-making mode: the mind
- lifestyle: organised

Similar personality types:

- the Practitioner
- the Administrator
- the Animator

Statistical data:

- *inspectors* constitute between six and ten per cent of the global community
- men predominate among *inspectors* (60 per cent)
- Switzerland is an example of a nation corresponding to the *inspector's* profile

Find out more!

The Inspector. Your Guide to the ISTJ Personality Type by Jaroslaw Jankowski

The Logician (INTP)

Life motto: Above all else, seek to discover the truths about the world.

Logicians are original, resourceful and creative. With a love for solving problems of a theoretical nature, they are analytical, quick-witted, enthusiastically disposed towards new concepts and have the ability to connect individual phenomena, educing general rules and theories from them. Logical, exact and inquiring, they are quick to spot incoherence and inconsistency.

Logicians are independent, sceptical of existing solutions and authorities, tolerant and open to new challenges. When immersed in thought, they will sometimes lose touch with the outside world.

The *logician's* four natural inclinations:

- source of life energy: the interior world

- mode of assimilating information: intuition
- decision-making mode: the mind
- lifestyle: spontaneous

Similar personality types:

- the Strategist
- the Innovator
- the Director

Statistical data:

- *logicians* constitute between two and three per cent of the global community;
- men predominate among *logicians* (80 per cent)
- India is an example of a nation corresponding to the *logician's* profile

Find out more!

The Logician. Your Guide to the INTP Personality Type by Jaroslaw Jankowski

The Mentor (INFJ)

Life motto: The world CAN be a better place!

Mentors are creative and sensitive. With their gaze fixed firmly on the future, they spot opportunities and potential imperceptible to others. Idealists and visionaries, they are geared towards helping people and are conscientious, responsible and, at one and the same time, courteous, caring and friendly. They strive to understand the mechanisms governing the world and view problems from a wide perspective.

Superb listeners and observers, *mentors* are characterised by their extraordinary empathy, intuition and trust of people and are capable of reading the feelings and emotions of others. They find criticism and conflict difficult to bear and can come across as enigmatic.

The *mentor's* four natural inclinations:

- source of life energy: the interior world
- mode of assimilating information: intuition
- decision-making mode: the heart
- lifestyle: organised

Similar personality types:

- the Idealist
- the Counsellor
- the Enthusiast

Statistical data:

- *mentors* constitute one per cent of the global community and are the most rarely occurring of the sixteen personality types
- women predominate among *mentors* (80 per cent)
- Norway is an example of a nation corresponding to the *mentor's* profile

Find out more!

The Mentor. Your Guide to the INFJ Personality Type by Jaroslaw Jankowski

The Practitioner (ISTP)

Life motto: Actions speak louder than words.

Practitioners are optimistic and spontaneous, with a positive approach to life. Reserved and independent, they hold true to their personal convictions and view external principles and norms with scepticism. They find abstract concepts and solutions for the future tiresome and would far rather roll up their sleeves and get to work on solving tangible and concrete problems.

Adapting well to new places and situations, they enjoy fresh challenges and risks and are capable of keeping a cool head in the face of threats and danger. Their general reticence and extreme reserve when it comes to expressing their opinions mean that other people may often find them impenetrable.

The *practitioner's* four natural inclinations:

- source of life energy: the interior world
- mode of assimilating information: via the senses
- decision-making mode: the mind
- lifestyle: spontaneous

Similar personality types:

- the Inspector
- the Animator
- the Administrator

Statistical data:

- *practitioners* constitute between six and nine per cent of the global community
- men predominate among *practitioners* (60 per cent)
- Singapore is an example of a nation corresponding to the *practitioner's* profile

Find out more!

The Practitioner. Your Guide to the ISTP Personality Type by Jaroslaw Jankowski

The Presenter (ESFP)

Life motto: Now is the perfect moment!

Presenters are optimistic, energetic and outgoing, with the ability to enjoy life and have fun to the full. Practical, flexible and spontaneous at one and the same time, they enjoy change and new experiences, coping badly with solitude, stagnation and routine.

With their liking for being at the centre of attention, they are natural-born actors and their speaking abilities arouse the interest and enthusiasm of their listeners. Focused as they are on the present moment, they will sometimes lose sight of their long-term aims and can also have problems with foreseeing the consequences of their actions.

The *presenter's* four natural inclinations:

- source of life energy: the exterior world
- mode of assimilating information: via the senses
- decision-making mode: the heart
- lifestyle: spontaneous

Similar personality types:

- the Advocate
- the Artist
- the Protector

Statistical data:

- *presenters* constitute between eight and thirteen per cent of the global community
- women predominate among *presenters* (60 per cent)
- Brazil is an example of a nation corresponding to the *presenter's* profile

Find out more!

The Presenter. Your Guide to the ESFP Personality Type by Jaroslaw Jankowski

The Protector (ISFJ)

Life motto: Your happiness matters to me.

Protectors are sincere, warm-hearted, unassuming, trustworthy and extraordinarily loyal. With their ability to perceive people's needs and their desire to help them, they will always put others first. Practical, well-organised and gifted with both an eye and a memory for detail, they are responsible, hard-working, patient, persevering and capable of seeing things through to the end.

Protectors set great store by tranquillity, stability and friendly relations with others and are skilled at building bridges between people. By the same token, they find conflict and criticism difficult to bear. Given their powerful sense of duty and their constant readiness to come to the aid of others, they can end up being used by people.

The *protector's* four natural inclinations:

- source of life energy: the interior world
- mode of assimilating information: via the senses
- decision-making mode: the heart
- lifestyle: organised

Similar personality types:

- the Artist
- the Advocate
- the Presenter

Statistical data:

- *protectors* constitute between eight and twelve per cent of the global population
- women predominate among *protectors* (70 per cent)
- Sweden is an example of a nation corresponding to the *protector's* profile

Find out more!

The Protector. Your Guide to the ISFJ Personality Type by Jaroslaw Jankowski

The Strategist (INTJ)

Life motto: I can certainly improve this.

Strategists are independent and outstandingly individualistic, with an immense seam of inner energy. Creative, inventive and resourceful, others perceive them as competent, self-assured and, at one and the same time, distant and enigmatic. No matter what they turn their attention to, they will always look at the bigger picture and they have a driving urge to improve the world around them and set it in order.

Well-organised, responsible, critical and demanding, they are difficult to knock off balance – and just as hard to please to the full. Reading the emotions and feelings of others is something they find very problematic.

The *strategist's* four natural inclinations:

- source of life energy: the interior world
- mode of assimilating information: intuition
- decision-making mode: the mind
- lifestyle: organised

Similar personality types:

- the Logician
- the Director
- the Innovator

Statistical data:

- *strategists* constitute between one and two per cent of the global community
- men predominate among *strategists* (80 per cent)
- Finland is an example of a nation corresponding to the *strategist's* profile

Find out more!

The Strategist. Your Guide to the INTJ Personality Type by Jaroslaw Jankowski

Additional information

The four natural inclinations

1. THE DOMINANT SOURCE OF LIFE
    ENERGY

    a. THE EXTERIOR WORLD
        People who draw their energy
        from outside. They need activity
        and contact with others and find
        being alone for any length of time
        hard to bear.

    b. THE INTERIOR WORLD
        People who draw their energy
        from their inner world. They need
        quiet and solitude and feel drained

when they spend any length of time in a group.

2. THE DOMINANT MODE OF ASSIMILATING INFORMATION

a. VIA THE SENSES

People who rely on the five senses and are persuaded by facts and evidence. They have a liking for methods and practices which are tried and tested and prefer concrete tasks and are realists who trust in experience.

b. VIA INTUITION

People who rely on the sixth sense and are driven by what they 'feel in their bones'. They have a liking for innovative solutions and problems of a theoretical nature and are characterised by a creative approach to their tasks and the ability to predict.

3. THE DOMINANT DECISION-MAKING MODE

a. THE MIND

People who are guided by logic and objective principles. They are critical and direct in expressing their opinions.

   b. THE HEART
People who are guided by their feelings and values. They long for harmony and mutual understanding with others.

4. THE DOMINANT LIFESTYLE

   a. ORGANISED
People who are conscientious and organised. They value order and like to operate according to plan.

   b. SPONTANEOUS
People who are spontaneous and value freedom of action. They live for the moment and have no trouble finding their feet in new situations.

The approximate percentage of each personality type in the world population

Personality Type:	Proportion:
• The Administrator (ESTJ):	10-13%
• The Advocate (ESFJ):	10-13%
• The Animator (ESTP):	6-10%
• The Artist (ISFP):	6-9%
• The Counsellor (ENFJ):	3-5 %
• The Director (ENTJ):	2-5%
• The Enthusiast (ENFP):	5-8%

- The Idealist (INFP):   1-4%
- The Innovator (ENTP):   3-5%
- The Inspector (ISTJ):   6-10%
- The Logician (INTP):   2-3%
- The Mentor (INFJ):   ca. 1%
- The Practitioner (ISTP):   6-9%
- The Presenter (ESFP):   8-13%
- The Protector (ISFJ):   8-12%
- The Strategist (INTJ):   1-2%

The approximate percentage of women and men of each personality type in the world population

Personality Type:	Women / Men:
The Administrator (ESTJ):	40% / 60%
The Advocate (ESFJ):	70% / 30%
The Animator (ESTP):	40% / 60%
The Artist (ISFP):	60% / 40%
The Counsellor (ENFJ):	80% / 20%
The Director (ENTJ):	30% / 70%
The Enthusiast (ENFP):	60% / 40%
The Idealist (INFP):	60% / 40%
The Innovator (ENTP):	30% / 70%
The Inspector (ISTJ):	40% / 60%
The Logician (INTP):	20% / 80%
The Mentor (INFJ):	80% / 20%
The Practitioner (ISTP):	40% / 60%
The Presenter (ESFP):	60% / 40%
The Protector (ISFJ):	70% / 30%
The Strategist (INTJ):	20% / 80%

Bibliography

- Arraj, Tyra & Arraj, James: *Tracking the Elusive Human, Volume 1: A Practical Guide to C.G. Jung's Psychological Types, W.H. Sheldon's Body and Temperament Types and Their Integration*, Inner Growth Books, 1988

- Arraj, James: *Tracking the Elusive Human, Volume 2: An Advanced Guide to the Typological Worlds of C. G. Jung, W.H. Sheldon, Their Integration, and the Biochemical Typology of the Future*, Inner Growth Books, 1990

- Berens, Linda V.; Cooper, Sue A.; Ernst, Linda K.; Martin, Charles R.; Myers, Steve; Nardi, Dario; Pearman, Roger R.; Segal, Marci; Smith, Melissa: *A. Quick Guide to the 16 Personality Types in Organizations: Understanding Personality Differences in the Workplace*, Telos Publications, 2002

- Geier, John G. & Downey, E. Dorothy: *Energetics of Personality*, Aristos Publishing House, 1989

- Hunsaker, Phillip L. & Alessandra, Anthony J.: *The Art of Managing People*, Simon and Schuster, 1986

- Jung, Carl Gustav: *Psychological Types (The Collected Works of C. G. Jung, Vol. 6)*, Princeton University Press, 1976

- Kise, Jane A. G.; Stark, David & Krebs Hirsch, Sandra: *LifeKeys: Discover Who You Are*, Bethany House, 2005

- Kroeger, Otto & Thuesen, Janet: *Type Talk or How to Determine Your Personality Type and Change Your Life*, Delacorte Press, 1988

- Lawrence, Gordon: *People Types and Tiger Stripes*, Center for Applications of Psychological Type, 1993

- Lawrence, Gordon: *Looking at Type and Learning Styles*, Center for Applications of Psychological Type, 1997

- Maddi, Salvatore R.: *Personality Theories: A Comparative Analysis*, Waveland, 2001

- Martin, Charles R.: *Looking at Type: The Fundamentals Using Psychological Type To Understand and Appreciate Ourselves and Others*, Center for Applications of Psychological Type, 2001

- Meier C.A.: Personality: *The Individuation Process in the Light of C. G. Jung's Typology*, Daimon Verlag, 2007

- Pearman, Roger R. & Albritton, Sarah: *I'm Not Crazy, I'm Just Not You: The Real Meaning of the*

Sixteen Personality Types, Davies-Black Publishing, 1997

- Segal, Marci: Creativity and Personality Type: *Tools for Understanding and Inspiring the Many Voices of Creativity*, Telos Publications, 2001
- Sharp, Daryl: Personality Type: *Jung's Model of Typology*, Inner City Books, 1987
- Spoto, Angelo: *Jung's Typology in Perspective*, Chiron Publications, 1995
- Tannen, Deborah: *You Just Don't Understand*, William Morrow and Company, 1990
- Thomas, Jay C. & Segal, Daniel L.: *Comprehensive Handbook of Personality and Psychopathology, Personality and Everyday Functioning*, Wiley, 2005
- Thomson, Lenore: *Personality Type: An Owner's Manual*, Shambhala, 1998
- Tieger, Paul D. & Barron-Tieger Barbara: *Just Your Type: Create the Relationship You've Always Wanted Using the Secrets of Personality Type*, Little, Brown and Company, 2000
- Von Franz, Marie-Louise & Hillman, James: *Lectures on Jung's Typology*, Continuum International Publishing Group, 1971

www.ingramcontent.com/pod-product-compliance
Lightning Source LLC
Chambersburg PA
CBHW031208020426
42333CB00013B/847